S OHO HOUSE was the home of Matthew Boulton for forty-three years until his death in 1809. Born in 1728, Boulton lived through a period of great technological and scientific change in which he played a key role, becoming one of England's pioneer industrialists, a man whom his friend Josiah Wedgwood described as 'The most complete manufacturer in metals in England'.

In 1761, needing a site to build his new Manufactory, Boulton paid £1,000 for the lease on Soho Mill, the house and land. Soho House, built c.1757, was valued at £300. The name 'Soho' is said to represent the call of a hunting horn on an inn-sign which was then nearby. When Boulton acquired the house the interior was unfinished. He had it completed, but not until 1766 did he and his second wife, Ann, make it their home. Their children, Anne and Matthew Robinson Boulton, were born at Soho.

▲ **The south front of Soho House today.**

▲ **James Wyatt's drawing of the north front** showing the proposed extension to Soho House, *1796*.

Until the end of his long life Matthew Boulton spent much time, thought and money improving the modest house, and its complex architectural history is still not fully understood. In the 1790s he had it extensively re-designed by the architect James Wyatt, with the present façade and a new service wing housing a library and domestic quarters, a scheme largely executed by Samuel Wyatt. The London interior designer Cornelius Dixon and the furniture maker James Newton were brought in to transform the house into a fashionable gentleman's residence where Boulton could entertain distinguished guests in style. Over the years he also created a substantial landscaped park surrounding his house and Manufactory.

Among the frequent guests at Soho were the members of the Lunar Society, one of the eighteenth century's foremost philosophical societies. This group met at one another's homes on or near the night of the full moon, so that they would have better light to travel home by afterwards. Over dinner they discussed their latest scientific ideas, often adjourning to the study afterwards for a few experiments or to peer down Boulton's microscope.

The Soho Manufactory and Soho Park disappeared long ago under later housing. Only Soho House survives, though its service wing was demolished at the end of the nineteenth century. Since then it has been, by turn, a private house, a vicarage, a girls' school, a hotel, an apprentices' hall of residence, and a police hostel.

In 1990 Birmingham Museums and Art Gallery set about restoring Soho House as closely as possible to its appearance c.1790, working largely from information in the Soho Archives in Birmingham City Archives. The house, which is Grade II* listed, opened to the public in October 1995.

▲ Pupils and teachers at **Birmingham Central High School for Girls**, Soho House, *c.1893.*

A.A.   APPOINTED   R.A.C.

Member of the
Residential Hotels Association of Great Britain

SOHO HALL HOTEL

SOHO AVENUE
HANDSWORTH
BIRMINGHAM, 19

◀ Tarriff card for **Soho Hall Hotel**, *c. 1945.* The portico was knocked down when a lorry backed into it during the wartime blackout, and was replaced by the canopy porch on this illustration. The portico was rebuilt during the *1950s.*

▲ **Soho House and park**, engraved by Francis Eginton for Stebbing Shaw's *History and Antiquities of the County of Stafford, 1798.*

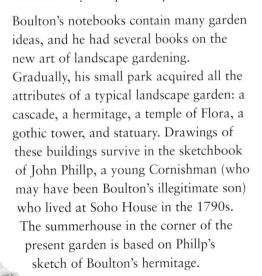

▼ **One of a pair of carved stone sphinxes** bought by Matthew Boulton for his garden in *1795.*

Having started with thirteen acres of land at Soho, Matthew Boulton eventually built up an estate of c.200 acres, where he created a park with gardens and a farm. The old Soho Mill Pool was enlarged to a sizeable lake, providing both water for the Manufactory and picturesque views.

Boulton's notebooks contain many garden ideas, and he had several books on the new art of landscape gardening. Gradually, his small park acquired all the attributes of a typical landscape garden: a cascade, a hermitage, a temple of Flora, a gothic tower, and statuary. Drawings of these buildings survive in the sketchbook of John Phillp, a young Cornishman (who may have been Boulton's illegitimate son) who lived at Soho House in the 1790s. The summerhouse in the corner of the present garden is based on Phillp's sketch of Boulton's hermitage.

Though he was clearly influenced by the ideas of the landscape gardeners, Boulton's park was very much his own creation. In 1795, contemplating it, he wrote:

No Forest, but a Garden neat
An easy Walk, a resting seat
Made from the barren Wast by me
Who planted every Flower and Tree...

▲ **A watercolour by John Phillp** showing Matthew Boulton's hermitage, *c.1795*. The hermitage was one of several buildings in the park; Boulton described it as 'a building adapted for contemplation in the prettiest part of my garden'.

Wyatt style

The façade of Soho House was re-designed by James Wyatt as part of the 1790s extension and alterations. The brick walls were clad in Welsh slate, and the pilasters and columned porch were added to give the building a neoclassical style. It was coated with a sand-textured paint, to give a stone-like finish. The new Wyatt wing was to the west, extending beyond the present small two-storey extension and across to where the neighbouring houses now stand.

When Soho House was re-modelled in the 1790s Boulton would have liked a grand entrance. Making the most of the small space, and by a clever use of proportion, the Wyatts transformed the hall into an elegant reception area, using marble pillars and pilasters and a decorative plaster cornice to create the illusion of a colonnaded ante-room at the rear, with alcoves either side of the Dining Room doors which probably held statues or pedestal vases.

Three pairs of mahogany and rosewood double doors lead to the Dining Room, the Vestibule, and the Breakfast Room. A bill of £51 15s for them survives, dated 1798. Some of the door furniture is original and was made at Soho. There is also a fourth door from the Hall. This was a 'jebb' door or hidden door used by servants to bring food quickly to the Dining Room. On the Hall side it is plastered so that it merges unobtrusively into the wall.

Matthew Boulton, ▶ by Lemuel Francis Abbott, oil, *1801*. It shows the manufacturer at the age of 73.

▼ **Design for the Hall floor-cloth,** *1799*.

The Hall floor was covered with a painted floor-cloth. Floor-cloths were the forerunners of linoleum, and were often used in areas where they would be easier to clean than carpets. They were made of canvas, painted with bold geometrical designs and thickly varnished. The present floorcloth has been painted from the design of the original, which survives along with correspondence complaining about its late delivery, and the bill for £19 4s 0d.

◀ **Ormolu and marble table** made at the Soho Manufactory, *c.1798*. It is believed to be the only one of its kind made at Soho. It has an ormolu-mounted gilt wood frieze, and ormolu legs.

▼ **Fragment of eighteenth-century wallpaper** found beneath many other layers.

The mahogany table is late eighteenth century, and is laid with Worcester porcelain from c.1770. The japanned and parcel gilt chairs are part of a set of twelve made for the Soho House Drawing Room by James Newton in 1798, at a cost of 42 shillings (£2 10p) each.

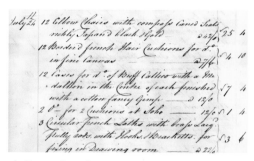

▲ **Extract from James Newton's furnishing accounts** detailing the elbow chairs.

The Breakfast Room is in the oldest part of Soho House, dating from c.1757. Like most rooms in the house, its windows retain their original wooden shutters. Eighteenth-century wallpaper found in the house has been reproduced.

The marble fireplace was installed in the 1790s. On the chimneypiece are three Wedgwood basalt vases, all late eighteenth century. Boulton liked this ware and wrote to Wedgwood in 1768 asking for

'Eligant Etruscan vases for my Cabinett, I being impatient as a Child'.

The side cabinet, originally from Belton House, Lincolnshire, was also made by James Newton c.1800, and is in rosewood and marble. The doors have gilt metal grilles with pleated silk backs.

Little was known about Boulton's carpets at Soho House, beyond the fact that they were Brussels weave (looped pile) and that they were 'made to plan', that is, fitted. In re-carpeting all the furnished rooms, documented eighteenth-century designs have been chosen. There was rather more evidence about the eighteenth-century curtains, in accounts from James Newton detailing fabrics, yardage, and borders, used as the basis for the present curtains.

The Drawing Room was the setting for after-dinner entertaining. Its bow window was added in the 1790s, along with a marble chimneypiece. A carved marble flower found in the garden proved to be from the 1790s' chimneypiece, and has been incorporated at the left-hand side of the present reproduction. On the chimneypiece are Blue John and ormolu candle vases made at Soho, c.1775, and a Wedgwood basalt bulb pot, late eighteenth century. The gilt wood mirror is c.1800.

The wallpapers reproduce exactly the eighteenth-century decorative scheme found in this room beneath later decorations.

The dominant object is the ormolu sidereal clock, made at the Soho Manufactory in 1771. The movement, by John Whitehurst of Derby, incorporates some of John Harrison's ideas developed for his marine chronometer in 1764. Boulton hoped his 'star clock' would fetch £275 at Christie & Ansell's in London, but it did not sell. In 1776 he sent it to St Petersburg, to the Empress Catherine. Unimpressed by its accuracy, the Court thought such an expensive clock ought at least to play tunes. In 1787 it came back to Soho. The pedestal was made for it by James Newton.

▲ **Detail of undated design drawing for the original fireplace**, probably *c.1797*

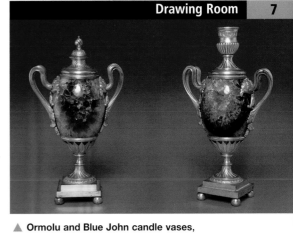

▲ **Ormolu and Blue John candle vases**, Boulton & Fothergill, *c.1775*.

Much of the furniture is by James Newton, including four of the 1798 Drawing Room chairs, the inlaid tortoiseshell and rosewood writing cabinets, c.1800, and the mahogany and rosewood table. The Carrara marble busts are left, Matthew Boulton, by John Flaxman, and right, James Watt, by Sir Francis Chantrey. The candelabra are Sheffield plate from the Soho Manufactory.

The pianoforte by Carolus Trute of London, c.1781, is probably a similar instrument to the one about which Boulton wrote to his daughter in 1801,

'Mrs Nicholson says there is a small Forte Piano sent to you about ten Days ago'.

Entertaining at Soho often included 'loyal songs' round the piano. The harp by Sebastian Erard is early nineteenth century.

◀ **Sidereal clock by Boulton & Fothergill**, ormolu case, *c.1771-2*.

The dining room is sometimes referred to as the 'Lunar Room', because members of the Lunar Society would dine here when it was Matthew Boulton's turn to host their meetings. Other guests ranged from the actress Sarah Siddons to the Russian Ambassador. James Wyatt created this stylish dining room in 1792, adding the shallow vaulted ceiling and the pillars and pilasters. The décor was devised by Cornelius Dixon and included painting the pillars and pilasters to resemble marble, with curtains hand-painted to match. This scheme has been followed in the restoration.

The bay window was another Wyatt addition, with its glazing bars made of 'Eldorado', an alloy of copper, iron and zinc developed by Boulton's friend the metallurgist James Keir. The centre and right-hand Eldorado frames survive today.

The marble chimneypiece reproduces the design of the original. The gilded mirror is attributed to Thomas Fentham, c.1805-10. On the chimneypiece stand a pair of ormolu perfume burners by Boulton & Fothergill, c.1771. These would often be used in a dining room to dispel food smells. The ormolu, bronze and marble candelabra, also by Boulton & Fothergill, c.1775, represent Apollo and Diana. Only two pairs are thought to have been made.

The extending mahogany dining table was made for this room by Benjamin Wyatt in 1798. The side table is the central section of it. The gothic-style chairs in oak with mahogany veneer are by Gillows of Lancaster, c.1784, and match closely the description of dining chairs which the furniture maker James Newton supplied to Boulton in the 1790s. In the alcoves either side of the fireplace are mahogany urns and pedestals, c.1785. One pedestal contains a plate warmer and the other is fitted for wine storage. The urns are lead-lined for storing ice.

▲ **The Dining Room**, often known as 'The Lunar Room' because members of the Lunar Society would dine here when it was Boulton's turn to host the meeting.

Double-spouted ▶ tea-urn, Sheffield plate, by Matthew Boulton, *c.1805-10*. This belonged to the Boulton family.

The 'silverware' is all Sheffield plate of Boulton's manufacture and includes candelabra and a pair of wine coolers. The blue and white earthenware serving dish is by George Bullock, c.1816.

▲ **Pair of ormolu perfume burners** by Boulton & Fothergill, *c.1771*.

Scientific guests

The object near the table is a reproduction of 'Dr Priestley's electrical machine'. Joseph Priestley, a member of the Lunar Society, devised this equipment for carrying out experiments. Producing electrical sparks and shocks was a popular eighteenth-century party trick, but Priestley's machine had a serious scientific purpose: the electrical spark it produced exploded a mixture of 'inflammable air' (hydrogen) and 'dephlogisticated air' (oxygen) in the glass tube, which produced droplets of water on the inside of the tube, demonstrating for the first time that water was a compound and not an element – one of many experiments carried out at Lunar Society meetings.

Meal-times in the past often differed from today. Once, when the botanist Sir Joseph Banks was expected to dinner, there was no sign of the guest at the usual dinner time of 4pm and '*at half past six ye Cook gave notice that the Venison would be overroasted,*' wrote Boulton. His daughter, Anne, fetched Banks's letter, and realised the great man was intending to come the following week. '*We therefore sat down to dinner at near 7 oClock & drank your health for giveing us a better dinner than we should otherwise have had,*' Boulton wrote to him.

◄ **'Diana', one of a pair of Apollo and Diana candelabra** by Boulton & Fothergill. Ormolu, bronze and marble, *c.1775*.

most of the time he lived at Soho House, instructing his daughter to take the readings when he was away from home.

The engraving of Matthew Boulton is by W. Sharp, after the 1801 portrait by Sir William Beechey, and was presented in memory of Major Eustace Robb, Boulton's great-great-grandson. The mezzotint of an Iron Forge is by Richard Earlom, after Joseph Wright of Derby, c.1773.

▼ **The Face of the Moon**, by John Russell, pastel, *c.1795*. Based on his observations through a telescope. The Lunar globe on the desk is also by Russell.

Т he first room along the ground-floor passage is Matthew Boulton's Study. The mahogany desk is by Gillows of Lancaster, c.1780. On the desk is one of James Watt's letter-copying machines, c.1780.

The mahogany chair is a Greek 'Klismos' design of c.1800 and is one of a pair originally from Soho House (the other one is at the Victoria and Albert Museum). '*Klismos*' chairs are frequently depicted on ancient Greek vases and painted reliefs; the word means '*throne*'.

The table is by James Newton. The diagonal barometer on the wall in the alcove is by John Whitehurst, c.1775. Boulton was interested in meteorology and kept meticulous weather records for

▲ **Matthew Boulton's list of his scientific equipment,** from his *1772* notebook.

oho House boasted 'all mod cons'. There were two Bramah patent flushing water closets, central heating, and a steam-heated bath. The first bathroom was in a wooden building with access from the house, but Boulton was not satisfied with it and had a bathroom and powdery made on the ground-floor corridor, using part of what had been the housekeeper's room. Here a bath was installed. According to an entry in Boulton's notebook the bath was 8'3" long, 5'9" wide, and 5'6" deep. It had to be filled from a well by the bucketful, which took some time, and then a nearby boiler was lit and steam was piped into the water to heat it.

Fossilry

The part of the former housekeeper's room which remained after the construction of the bathroom was initially turned into a rear entrance hall. Later it became a small room to house Boulton's fossil and mineral collection. The collection had been in one of the buildings in the Park, but as he grew older, bringing it indoors would have had obvious attractions.

Boulton had the mahogany cabinets built to house the collection. Each cabinet contains forty specimen drawers. The Sheffield plate lamp is an Argand lamp, made at Soho c.1800. This was a type of oil lamp, named after its Swiss inventor. The mahogany barometer is by Robert Masefield of Birmingham, c.1767. The terrestrial globe is papier maché, eighteenth century.

On the bookshelf is a Bible in the Baskerville typeface. John Baskerville was a contemporary and great friend of Matthew Boulton's.

The portrait is of Francis Eginton, by James Millar. Eginton (1737-1805) was a stained glass painter who worked for Boulton before becoming independent. He was the painter of the altar window at St Paul's Church in the Jewellery Quarter.

◄ **Matthew Boulton's Fossilry,** constructed and furnished to house his fossil and mineral collection.

▲ **Design from the Boulton pattern books for an Argand lamp,** similar to the Sheffield plate lamp on the mineral cabinet.

▲ **Extract from Matthew Boulton's notebook** giving the measurements of his bath.

When the now-demolished service wing was built in the 1790s, with the new kitchen and other domestic offices, the former kitchen became the Housekeeper's Room. None of the original fittings for this room survived, but the fitted cupboards have been copied from drawings by John Phillp, who also sketched some of the servants at work.

▲ **The Soho House butler at work**, drawn by John Phillp in 1799. This was probably Jervis Foster, who was suspected of being involved in an attempted wages robbery at the Manufactory the following year and was paid off and dismissed.

In the eighteenth century the 'family' at a house like this was assumed to include the servants. Calculating his tax liability in 1801, Boulton listed four male servants including Joseph Brook, 'John ye Boy', 'W[illia]m my Man', and a gardener, and three women servants, including the housekeeper, chambermaid and cook.

Cellars

The Cellars run under the whole building. Original slate wine-racking remains at one end, and Boulton's notebooks contain lists of '*Ale & Barrells in my Celle*r'.

Beside the stairs which lead out of the cellar is the cockle stove. This is a stove in which the fire is enclosed in a box, or cockle. Air coming into contact with the surfaces of the cockle was heated by the fire inside. The heated air passed along a network of ducts, to emerge around the house, through grilles in hearths or through the holes in the stair risers. This central heating system dates from the 1790s and is thought to be the first successful attempt to heat a large house by ducted hot air since Roman times.

▲ The original slate wine racks in the cellar.

▲ **'Ale & Barrells in my Celler'** - one of Matthew Boulton's numerous lists.

The holes in the stair ▶ risers are part of the eighteenth-century central heating system.

Matthew Boulton's daughter, Anne (1768-1829), lived at Soho House until after her brother's marriage in 1817, when she set up her own home at Thornhill House in Handsworth. She never married.

Anne and her father were close, writing to each other regularly when he was away from home on business. From childhood, Anne (or 'Nanney', as her father generally called her) had some kind of disability which made walking uncomfortable, but it did not prevent her travelling to visit friends, or her father when he was in London or Cornwall. At ten she went away to school in Richmond, near London, for a time. Music was important to her and there are bills for sheet music, tuition, and tuning a harpsichord and a pianoforte.

Anne's rooms on the first floor have been furnished appropriately. The Dressing Room and Powdery (where one of Soho House's two Bramah patent flushing water-closets was installed) would have been used by Anne and female guests to dress, powder wigs and faces, and prepare themselves for social evenings downstairs.

◀ **Thomas Rowlandson's** ***The Dressing Room*** *(c.1790).* For a fashionable and well-to-do young woman, an outing or a social evening in a Drawing Room required careful attention to hair and dress, often with the help of a maid.

The small day-bed in the dressing-room is of japanned wood, c.1805. The side cabinet of the same period is also in japanned wood, with silk panels in the doors. Pictures in here include *The Pilgrim*, by Sir William Hamilton, oil, late eighteenth century.

flower holder, c.1790, and a pair of Wedgwood jasperware vases, c.1810.

The two japanned elbow chairs are part of the 1798 Drawing Room set by James Newton, and the gilt wood mirror frame is early nineteenth century.

Pictures in the room include C.F. Von Breda's oil portrait of Mrs Joseph Priestley, 1793. Joseph Priestley and his wife were friends of the Boultons but were forced to flee Birmingham after the riots of 1791. The Priestleys emigrated to America in 1794.

▲ **The fanlight above the door** is of 'Eldorado', an experimental alloy of copper, iron and zinc devised by Boulton's friend James Keir.

Anne Boulton's sitting room, with its delicate 'Eldorado' metal fanlight over the door, was furnished with satinwood furniture which would have been light and warm-looking in this tiny but sunny room at the front of the house. In re-furnishing the room, care has been taken to achieve the same effect.

The sofa, japanned and gilded in the manner of George Hepplewhite, is c.1800. The satinwood secretaire, c.1800, has glazed doors and is fitted with pigeon holes and drawers, and a 'secret' kneehole drawer. It came from Brynbella and is thought to have belonged to Mrs Hester Thrale, a fashionable society hostess and close friend of Dr Johnson before her marriage to Gabriel Piozzi. On the secretaire are a Wedgwood jasperware

▲ **Mrs Joseph Priestley,** by C.F. von Breda, oil on canvas, *1793.*

▲ **One of Matthew Boulton's London shopping lists** which includes 'some beautyfull sentimental prints'. These were popular at the time and examples are to be seen in Miss Boulton's sitting room and bedroom.

Sheffield plate colza ▶ **oil lamp** by Matthew Boulton & Plate Co., *c.1820.*

▼ **Detail of plaster cornice in Miss Boulton's bedroom,** previously obliterated by many layers of paint.

nne Boulton's bedroom was divided into two smaller rooms in the 1960s. Now restored to its original size, it has been fitted with a reproduction fireplace. The decorative plaster cornice emerged from thick layers of white paint which had completely concealed its pattern.

The mahogany bedposts are late eighteenth century. The remaining parts of the bed and hangings are modern reproductions. The bed steps are mahogany, c.1800, as is the side table attributed to James Newton. Newton also made the pair of japanned and gilt chairs. The mahogany chest of drawers dates from 1765.

On the table is a bulb stand by John Turner, Staffordshire, late eighteenth century, and a Sheffield plate 'colza' (rape-seed oil) lamp by

Matthew Boulton & Plate Co. Another bulb pot and stand, in Chinese porcelain, c.1800, is on the chest of drawers.

The pictures include a mezzotint of Georgiana, Duchess of Devonshire, by Valentine Green after Joshua Reynolds.

This room was originally Matthew Boulton's library, and the oldest wallpaper found in the house, dating from this time, was found behind the built-in cupboard to the left of the fireplace. The marble fireplace is original, having been cleaned of many coats of white paint.

◀ **Fragment of mid-eighteenth century wallpaper**, found behind the fitted cupboards in Matthew Boulton's bedroom. It probably dates from when Boulton used this room as his library, before the 1790s extension was built.

When Boulton had the house extended in the 1790s the new wing included a much larger library, and from then on he used this room as his bedroom. It would have been here where he received Nelson when the naval hero visited Birmingham in 1802 and Boulton was too unwell to conduct him round the Soho Manufactory personally.

◀ **Matthew Boulton,** by C.F. Von Breda, oil on canvas, *1792*.

▲ **John Phillp's design for library shelving** to go in Boulton's new library in the extension.

The mahogany four-poster bed is eighteenth century, with modern hangings. The chest of drawers, also mahogany, is c.1770. The wing chair is from the Birmingham workshop of George Carr and is dated on the frame April 1753; the upholstery is modern.

The side table, c.1770, belonged to the Birmingham printer John Baskerville (1706-78), one of Boulton's oldest friends.

On the wall near the bed are prints of engravings of Soho House and the Soho Manufactory, done by Francis Eginton for Stebbing Shaw's *History and Antiquities of the County of Stafford* (1798).

The most important picture in the room is the 1792 oil portrait of Matthew Boulton by C.F. Von Breda. This shows Boulton at the height of his success and represents his various interests. In the background is the Soho Manufactory, while on the table near him are mineral specimens, and he holds a magnifying glass and a medal.

▲ **Boulton's diary entry recording Lord Nelson's visit.**

Three of the first-floor rooms are used for displays relating to the Boulton family, the history of Soho House, the Soho Mint and the products of the Soho Manufactory

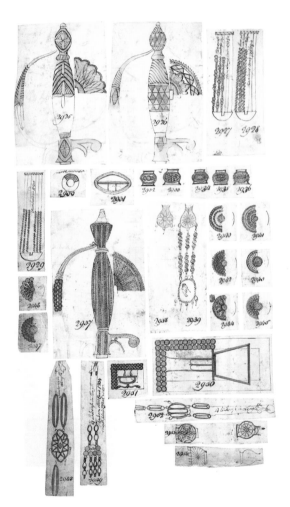

▲ **Designs for cut-steel buckles, buttons, jewellery and sword hilts,** from the Boulton & Fothergill pattern books.

[handwritten letter]

▲ **Extract from a letter from Matthew Boulton to his wife, Ann, in** *1763*, in which he tells her that he has presented one of his sword hilts to Prince Edward, who wore it to the play later that night.

▲ **Obverse and reverse of a 'cartwheel' penny** struck at Boulton's Soho Mint in *1797*. Boulton worked long and hard to get the contract for the British copper coinage, having built a modern mint at Soho.

▲ **Sugar bowl,** silver and silver-gilt, by Matthew Boulton *1789*.

Sugar, brought in from the Caribbean, became widely available during the eighteenth century (annual consumption in Britain rose from 23,000 tons in 1700 to 245,000 tons in 1800). Sugar containers became a decorative addition to the table.

◀ **Bacchanalian vase**, Boulton & Fothergill, *c.1776-8*, ormolu and white marble. Designed to hold essence or perfume, the design of this vase was based on the antique Gaeta vase created by the Greek sculptor Salpion, now in the National Museum, Naples, but in the eighteenth century in use as a font in the cathedral at Gaeta.

▲ **Neoclassical-style silver coffee pot and stand** by Boulton & Fothergill, *1769*, one of very few pieces of known Boulton silver to bear the Chester Assay Office mark. Boulton vowed never to go into large-scale silverware production unless Birmingham was granted its own Assay Office. After a two-year campaign by Boulton and others, the Birmingham Assay Office opened in 1773.

The Buckle-Maker's Son

▲ **Matthew Boulton at 42, by J.S.C. Schaak,** *1770.*

Matthew Boulton was born in Birmingham on 14 September 1728. His parents were Matthew Boulton senior of Birmingham and Christiana Piers of Chester. Matthew Boulton senior was a steel buckle- and toy-maker in the Snow Hill area of Birmingham. 'Birmingham toys' were not children's playthings but small decorative items for personal use, such as buckles, buttons, snuff boxes, chatelaines and other trinkets. 'Toy' making was a rapidly growing industry in the town.

The young Matthew Boulton attended a school in Deritend and joined his father's business about 1745. In 1749 he married

Mary Robinson, the daughter of a well-to-do Lichfield mercer, Luke Robinson, and his wife Dorothy Babington. Boulton and his wife were distantly related.

So far as is known, Matthew and Mary had three daughters, Dorothea, Anne (or Anna), and Maria, but by 1753 all three children were dead. In August 1759 their mother Mary also died. Scarcely had Matthew Boulton buried his wife when his father, Matthew Boulton senior, died. At the time of his death, Boulton senior seems to have been living at Sarehole Farm, Birmingham.

Matthew Boulton now took over the business in Snow Hill. He also began to think about remarriage, and in June 1760 married his late wife's sister, Ann Robinson, whom he referred to affectionately as 'Nanny' or 'Nancy'.

▲ **Cut steel shoe buckle with leather insert, by** Boulton & Smith, typical of the goods being produced by Boulton's father's business in Snow Hill, and later at the Soho Manufactory.

My Dear

[handwritten letter]

▲ **Letter from Matthew Boulton** to his second wife, Ann Robinson, about staff.

Though not then illegal, marriage to a dead wife's sister was certainly frowned upon by the Church, and the wedding took place well away from home, at St. Mary's, Rotherhithe, London.

The couple began their married life at Snow Hill, and it was not until 1766 that they made their home at Soho House. Here their children were born, Anne in 1768, and Matthew Robinson in 1770. Boulton proved an affectionate and indulgent father, referring to his children by the pet-names 'the Fair Maid of the Mill' and 'the General of Soho'. He had been introduced to the Royal children, he wrote to his wife from London in 1772,

but though charming, they did not compare with little 'Nanney' and Matt.

Although Boulton's own formal education had finished quite early, he took pleasure in learning and set about collecting a library which would not only broaden his knowledge but also be of practical use, ranging from the classics to *The Art of Assaying*, to Sterne's *Tristram Shandy*. He was especially interested in all branches of natural philosophy (what we would now call science) and his notebooks contain many accounts of experiments performed and scientific equipment wanted or purchased. He planned a 'hobby-horsery' with laboratories and an observatory, and certainly had a telescope mounted on the roof of Soho House.

▲ **'Dash'**, the Boulton family dog, sketched by John Phillp in *1801*.

▲ **Matthew Robinson Boulton** at three years old, by Jean Etienne Liotard.

knowledge of French, German, mathematics, science – and dancing.

Boulton's wife died in 1783, perhaps from some kind of stroke. She was found dead in a pool in the grounds of Soho House, but had not drowned, and letters suggest that she had been having minor fits of some kind for a while before her death. Young Anne was fifteen when her mother died, and from then on began to help her father entertain the many distinguished visitors to Soho House.

Despite poor health in his later years Matthew Boulton continued to take an interest in the business, his garden, and science – at seventy-three his daughter had to beg him in January '*to set aside the telescope 'till warmer weather'*. He died at Soho House in August 1809, shortly before his eighty-first birthday.

After their father's death Matt and Anne continued to live at Soho House. Matt bought a country estate at Great Tew in Oxfordshire in 1815, for holiday use. In 1817 he married Mary Anne Wilkinson, niece of John Wilkinson the ironmaster. During the twelve years of their marriage they had eight children.

With a new mistress in charge at Soho House, Anne Boulton left to set up her own home, not far away at Thornhill

It is not surprising, therefore, that he paid close attention to his children's education. Anne was sent to a school in Richmond at the age of ten, and later continued her education at home. Her brother Matt received an education designed to make a gentleman of him and also equip him for eventually taking over the business. He went to schools in Twickenham and later near Colchester, where his tutor had to keep reminding him not to drop his 'Hs', before being sent to Versailles and Paris to acquire a

▲ **Part of a design for alterations to Anne Boulton's home,** Thornhill House, *1822*.

▼ **The Boulton family coat of arms,** engraved on the silver tea-vase displayed in the case in the Museum Room (metalwares). The first quarter represents the arms of Boulton granted on his appointment as High Sherriff of Staffordshire, the anchor representing the symbol of Birmingham Assay Office. The arms in the remaining quarters are those of the Lowth and Babington families from which Boulton was descended, and the Robinson family into which he married.

House. Anne never married. She died in 1829 at the age of sixty-one. Her sister-in-law died the same year. Matthew Robinson Boulton died in 1842. His elder son, Matthew Piers Watt Boulton, looked upon Tew Park as home. By the middle of the nineteenth century the Boulton family was no longer in residence at Soho House, and M.P.W. Boulton began dividing up his grandfather's park as plots for building many of the Victorian properties that now surround Soho House. With the death of M.P.W. Boulton's son, Matthew Ernest Boulton, in 1914, the male line from Matthew Boulton died out.

The Soho Manufactory

The 'Most Complete Manufacturer in Metals in England'.

Matthew Boulton inherited the family buckle and button business in 1759, and quickly decided that expansion was the way forward. The workshop in Snow Hill in Birmingham town centre was not big enough, so in 1761 he bought the lease on the site at Soho, in Handsworth. That same summer he began to build the Soho Manufactory. By 1765 the building was complete, at a cost of some £10,000 – well above the architects' estimates, but now Boulton had the space, the workers and the equipment to expand his product range.

He continued to produce the old family range of buttons and buckles, but to them he added cut steel jewellery and sword hilts. Then he began to manufacture tableware in Sheffield plate. Sheffield plate wares were made from silver-on-copper sheet, so that they had the outward appearance of silver, at a fraction of the price of goods made

The Soho Manufactory, showing the 'principal building' with its ranges of workshops behind.
Published in J. Bissett's Magnificent Directory, *1800*.

entirely of sterling silver. Elegantly designed Sheffield plate satisfied a desire for 'family silver' from a growing middle class.

There was a wealthier clientele who could afford sterling silver, and Boulton determined to supply them, too. The same or similar designs could be used, and the same craftsmen. The stumbling block was the hallmarking laws, which required all sterling silver wares to be assayed, or tested, and hallmarked at an assay office. In the mid 1760s the nearest assay offices to Birmingham were at Chester and London, both several days' journey away. Boulton sent a few wares to Chester for hallmarking but was frustrated by the delays and the risks of damage or theft en route, so in 1771 he began a campaign for an assay office in Birmingham. After two years the campaign succeeded, and in 1773 Birmingham Assay Office opened, with Matthew Boulton the first to register his mark there and to bring a large consignment of goods for assaying and hallmarking.

In addition to silverware, Boulton began to produce fashionable ormolu (gilded) decorative objects, such as clocks, candelabra and perfume burners, often combining the richly gilded metal parts with colourful stone, such as Blue John.

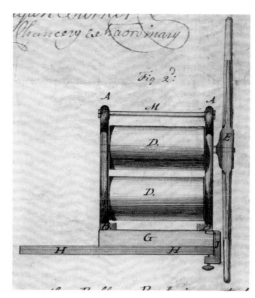

▲ **Patent drawing for a letter copying machine** by James Watt & Co., *c.1780*. This is a larger version of the copy-press on the Study desk. Watt devised the world's first copier to produce file copies of correspondence, using a special slow-drying ink to write letters and translucent absorbent tissue paper to produce an impression of the writing. Many such copy-press letters survive in the Soho Archives.

◀ **Ormolu candelabra designs** from the Boulton & Fothergill pattern books. Among the designs are those for the Apollo and Diana candelabra in the Dining Room.

▲ **Extract from a letter from Matthew Boulton** in which he says his partner John Fothergill, who is on a sales trip, plans to leave St Petersburg 'by the first sledges that go to Narva, Mettau and Riga'.

Boulton's target customers for these decorative goods were the aristocracy and fashionable society, and he spent much time and effort cultivating their acquaintance. The Soho Manufactory, with its hundreds of workers (Boulton claimed 1,000) and the novelty of its machines in perpetual production, became an essential stop on the tours of wealthy travellers from all over Britain and Europe. The number of these visitors grew so great that Boulton had a tea-house built in the grounds of the Manufactory. Here his visitors were entertained to tea or wine and cakes after their factory tour, and had the opportunity to see a showroom and buy a souvenir of their visit. Many of the visitors made donations to the Soho Insurance Society, one of the first 'sick club' schemes in the world, to which all workers contributed and from which they received money if they were off work through sickness.

The Soho Manufactory quickly became a famous showpiece, but Boulton, quick to see potential, was about to assure its place in history. Recognising the importance of James Watt's development work on the steam-engine, in 1774 he persuaded Watt to move from Scotland to Birmingham and join him in the business. The Boulton & Watt partnership was formally constituted in 1775. Two years later, another Scotsman, William Murdoch, a fine and inventive engineer, also joined the team.

▲ **William Murdoch,** *(1754-1839),* by John Graham Gilbert, R.S.A.

Over the next 30 years Boulton & Watt engines were installed in many countries. They drove spinning machines, pumped out mines, powered coining presses and sugar-cane crushers. Wherever there was

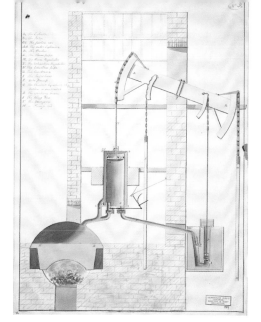

▲ **Drawing of a Boulton and Watt pumping engine,** made for patent trials, *c.1790*.

▲ **Mezzotint of James Watt,** the Scottish engineer who joined Boulton as his business partner in *1775*.

a need for power, Watt could devise an application for the steam engine. In 1776 Boulton observed to Dr. Johnson's friend James Boswell,

'I sell here, Sir, what all the world desires to have - POWER.'

By the 1790s demand for steam engines was such that a second site was acquired in Smethwick, where the Soho Foundry was built to produce the large cast parts for these engines.

Boulton meanwhile turned his attention to coining. Counterfeit coins had long been a problem in Britain, and he set his heart on developing techniques to

produce an improved British copper coinage which would be more difficult to counterfeit. In 1797 he won the government contract for copper coins including the famous 'cartwheel' penny. Two years later he won the contract to supply the Royal Mint with coining machinery.

After Boulton's death in 1809 his son, Matthew Robinson Boulton, continued to run the business, in partnership with James Watt's son, James Watt Junior. By the time of M.R. Boulton's death in 1842 the business was much reduced, various parts of it having been sold off as independent concerns.

Today nothing remains above ground of the Soho Manufactory. It lasted 100 years, being demolished in 1862-3.

The Lunar Society

The eighteenth century, the period of the Enlightenment, saw a surge of interest in scientific subjects, and in many towns and cities philosophical societies were formed, and people flocked to attend lectures and demonstrations. Some of these societies had a large membership and met in halls and lecture theatres. However a society of a slightly different kind began to take shape in Birmingham. Though small in numbers, it was to become one of the century's most influential philosophical societies.

It was around 1766 when the physician Dr. Erasmus Darwin invited Matthew Boulton and his friend Dr William Small to join him at his Lichfield home for dinner and a little scientific conversation. These early meetings formed the basis of what became known as the Lunar Society. The Society took its name from the fact that

▲ **Frontispiece from a French book** on balloons by Faujas de St Fond. The book was in Boulton's library.

▲ **'A chemical lecture at the Royal Institution'**, *1802* cartoon by Gillray.

members met around the night of the full moon, so that they might have better light by which to travel home. The members, who had wide-ranging interests, took it in turns to meet in one another's homes, often at Soho House, where Boulton was a hospitable host and kept a good table.

It was a select band - there were never more than fourteen members, and they were never all together at once, yet they comprised some of the outstanding minds of the period, and made major contributions to scientific understanding.

◀ **'A Philosopher giving a Lecture on the Orrery'**, by Joseph Wright of Derby. Wright was friendly with several of the Lunar Society members and took an interest in their experiments.

Of the fourteen, ten were Fellows of the Royal Society, and four were also Fellows of the Linnaean Society. Between them they were in correspondence with many other leading thinkers across Europe.

Some of the most important work was Priestley's. He discovered the power of plants to restore air by converting the carbon dioxide breathed out by animals into oxygen (which he termed '*dephlogisticated air*'). Watt and Priestley demonstrated for the first time that water was a compound, and not (as had been thought up till then) an element. This was also a major scientific breakthrough. In the course of his work Priestley found a way to impregnate water with carbon dioxide, an idea taken up by one Jacob Schweppe who began supplying the philosophers of Soho with fizzy water by the cartload.

The Lunar Society continued to meet, with the sons of Boulton, Watt and Galton adding to its membership, until the early years of the nineteenth century, but by 1813 most of the older members had died or left. In a poignant little ceremony on 8 August that year, Matthew Robinson Boulton, James Watt Junior, the son of Samuel Galton and Capt. James Keir drew lots for the Society's library of scientific books. Young Galton won the draw, and sent a cart to Soho House to carry away the books, which have not been heard of since.

B.
Whoever draws the Letter B is entitled to no prize of the Scientific Books

▲ **The end of the Lunar Society:** the 'winning ticket' in the draw for the Society's library of scientific books, *1813.*

Members of the Lunar Society:

Dr Erasmus Darwin, M.D., F.R.S., F.L.S. (1731-1802): physician, botanist, zoologist, poet, and grandfather of Charles Darwin. He was thinking along evolutionary lines long before his grandson shocked the world with *The Origin of Species*. In 1794 Erasmus Darwin wrote:

'*Would it be too bold to imagine, that in the great length of time, since the earth began to exist, perhaps millions of ages before the commencement of the history of mankind… that all warm-blooded animals have arisen from one living filament…?*'

He was genial, inventive, and had a gargantuan appetite, always travelling with a large hamper of food in his coach.

▲ **Dr. Erasmus Darwin, by Joseph Wright of Derby.**

Dr William Small, M.D. (1734-1775): a physician, he trained at Aberdeen before going to Virginia, where he became tutor in mathematics and natural philosophy at the William and Mary College at Williamsburg. One of his students was Thomas Jefferson, later third president of the United States. Small arrived in Birmingham in 1766, bearing a letter of introduction to Matthew Boulton from Benjamin Franklin.

▲ **Dr. William Small**

Matthew Boulton, F.R.S. (1728-1809): A button and buckle maker who built the Soho Manufactory and became one of Britain's greatest pioneer industrialists and entrepreneurs, Boulton's interest in science dated back to his youth – his early notebooks are packed with notes on chemistry and biology. He had an assortment of scientific instruments including a Dollond microscope. The grounds of Soho House included an observatory and a fossilry, both of which were transferred into the house in his later years.

Dr William Withering, M.D., F.R.S., F.L.S. (1741-1799): Edinburgh-trained, he was the physician at Birmingham's first General Hospital, founded in 1779. A keen botanist, he developed the medicinal use of digitalis from foxgloves.

James Watt, LL.D., F.R.S.(1736-1819): began his working life as a scientific instrument maker at Glasgow University and also became a surveyor on canal projects. He turned his attention to the steam engine, devising many improvements. Boulton invited him to join him in Birmingham in 1774.

Samuel Galton Jnr, F.R.S., F.L.S. (1753-1832): a Birmingham gun-maker and a Quaker - until the Society of Friends disowned him for '*fabricating and selling the instruments of war*'. He proved that the seven colours of the spectrum are all made from the three primary colours.

John Whitehurst, F.R.S. (1713-1788): a clock and scientific instrument maker from Derby. He made the movement of Boulton's great sidereal clock in the drawing room. He was also interested in geology and wrote a book on the formation of the earth.

Dr Jonathan Stokes, M.D., F.L.S. (1755-1831): a physician with a practice in Stourbridge, he classified plants useful to medicine and was interested in geology and botany.

Richard Lovell Edgeworth (1744-1817): like other much-travelled members of the Lunar Society, he detested being jolted on the rough roads and worked to improve the design of carriages. He was also interested in accurate land measurement and designed a land-measuring machine. He collaborated with his daughter, Maria, on a book on education for girls.

Thomas Day (1748-1789): a well-to-do young man who became friends with Edgeworth at Oxford. Not a scientist himself, he was better known as the author of a children's book, *Sandford and Merton*, and for his anti-slavery publications.

Dr Joseph Priestley, LL.D., F.R.S. (1733-1804): a Yorkshire weaver's son, he came to Birmingham in 1781 as a Unitarian Minister. By that time he had written books on electricity, light, colour, optics, and chemistry. In 1791 his house at Fair Hill, Sparkbrook, was burned by a mob which suspected him of sympathising with the French Revolution. All his scientific books, papers and equipment were destroyed, but Priestley escaped to London and later emigrated to America, where he remained very homesick for Birmingham and his scientific friends.

DOCTOR PHLOGISTON,
The PRIESTLEY politician or the
Political "Priest"!

Josiah Wedgwood, F.R.S. (1730-1795): interested in chemistry, dyes and soils - understandable for the man who was to become perhaps the world's greatest potter. He was also an enthusiastic early promoter of canals, an ideal way to transport fragile pottery. Wedgwood is regarded by some historians as an associate of the Lunar Society rather than as a member.

Capt. James Keir, F.R.S. (1735-1820): he left the army to concentrate on his scientific interests including chemistry and metallurgy. He translated a French Dictionary of Chemistry into English, and took an interest in the technical problems of the other manufacturing members of the Lunar Society. He was himself a manufacturer, with a glassworks at Stourbridge and a chemical works at Tipton.

Revd. Robert Augustus Johnson, F.R.S. (1745-1799): the least-known member of the Lunar Society. There is no published record of his work, though he is known to have had an interest in chemistry.

◀ **'Doctor Phlogiston,'** a 1791 cartoon of Joseph Priestley.

Matthew Boulton and Soho House - A Chronology

1728	Birth of Matthew Boulton.
1745	MB joins father's buckle and button business.
1749	Marries Mary Robinson.
1757c.	Soho House built.
1759	Death of Matthew Boulton's wife and father.
1760	Boulton marries Ann Robinson.
1761	Boulton leases 13 acres including Soho House.
1762-4	Soho Manufactory built.
1766	Matthew and Ann Boulton move into Soho House.
1768	Birth of Boulton's daughter, Anne Boulton.
1770	Birth of Boulton's son, Matthew Robinson Boulton.
1775	Boulton enters into partnership with James Watt.
1790	Soho House remodelled.
1809	Death of Matthew Boulton.
1815	M.R. Boulton buys country estate at Great Tew, Oxfordshire.
1817	M.R. Boulton marries Mary Anne Wilkinson.
1820	Birth of Matthew Piers Watt Boulton, 1st son of M.R. Boulton.
1842	Death of M.R. Boulton.
1850s	Boulton family now resident at Great Tew.
1860	Soho House a vicarage. Part of the Wyatts' extension demolished.
1862-3	Soho Manufactory demolished.
1893	Soho House a girls' school.
1894	Death of M.P.W. Boulton.
1903	Remainder of extension demolished.
1921	Soho House a hotel.
1955	Soho House a hall of residence for GEC apprentices.
1964	Soho House a police hostel.
1990	Birmingham City Council acquires Soho House.
1995	Soho House opens to the public.

The Archives of Soho

The restoration of Soho House was achieved with the help of research carried out in the Archives of Soho, held in Birmingham City Archives at the City's Central Library. This unrivalled collection of original documents covers the period from the middle of the eighteenth until virtually the end of the nineteenth centuries, and is one of the foremost resources on the period of the early Industrial Revolution, consulted by scholars from all over the world. There are three main collections: the Matthew Boulton Papers, the Boulton & Watt Papers, and the James Watt Papers. Between them they comprise over 250,000 documents, ranging from household bills, family letters and notebooks, to technical drawings for steam engines and designs for silverware. During 1999-2003 the archives were re-catalogued in a project funded in part by the Heritage Lottery Fund. The papers are available for public consultation. For more information, telephone 0121 303 4217.

Further reading

Delieb, Eric: *The Great Silver Manufactory* (London, 1971)
Dickinson, H.W: *Matthew Boulton* (Cambridge 1936, republished Leamington Spa, 1999)
Goodison, Nicholas: *Matthew Boulton: Ormolu* (Christie's Books, London, 2002)
Schofield, R.E.: *The Lunar Society of Birmingham* (Oxford, 1963)
Uglow, Jenny: *The Lunar Men* (London, 2002)

Acknowledgments

Birmingham Museums & Art Gallery acknowledges with gratitude the help of English Heritage, the Museums and Galleries Commission and the European Regional Development Fund, who supported the restoration of Soho House. In addition, important acquisitions have been made for the house thanks to the generosity of many organisations and individuals, in particular the National Art Collections Fund, Resource/V&A Purchase Grant Fund, the Lunar Society, the Heritage Lottery Fund, the Baring Foundation, the Esmee Fairbairn Charitable Trust, the Pilgrim Trust, TSB Plc, the J.Paul Getty Junior Charitable Trust, Sir Nicholas Goodison, the Edward Cadbury Charitable Trust, the J. and L.A. Cadbury Trust, Birmingham Assay Office, the John Feeney Charitable Trust, the Goldsmiths' Company, the Roughley Charitable Trust, the Charles Henry Foyle Trust, the Leche Trust, the George Henry Collins Charity, the Birmingham Common Good Trust, the Welconstruct Community Fund, the Birmingham Association of Mechanical Engineers, the Friends of Birmingham Museums and Art Gallery, and others too numerous to list.